I Must Share
That My Brother
May Live

by
Jeri Angela Knox

Mountain Top Books, Inc.

Please direct all correspondence and book orders to:
Mountain Top Books, Incorporated
1830 Knoll Drive
Oxon Hill, MD 20745

Library of Congress Catalog Card Number 91-91303
ISBN Number: 1-880679-00-0

2nd Edition

Logo by: Bruce Colbert, By His Spirit, Inc.

Published by Mountain Top Books, Incorporated
Oxon Hill, Maryland

Printed in the United States of America

Dear God:

Thank you!

Love,

Angie

Table Of Contents

i

Table Of Contents

Table Of Contents

Table Of Contents

I Must Share That My Brother May Live

I saw a man the other day,
His condition made me look away.
His clothes were torn and his body had a smell;
I'm sure he had a story he didn't care to tell.
He had turned to the street for living,
Getting his food from middle class giving.
I had decided long ago not to interfere,
Let those people get themselves back into gear.

Just as I was walking by,
He accidently caught my eye.
I saw feelings that are easy to recognize;
Anguish and despair, this came as no surprise.
But what caught me off guard was how quickly was etched,
An indelible picture as though artistically sketched.
I am never bothered by what I see,
But in him I saw a lot of me.

As I pondered his weathered face,
I thought there go I except for God's grace.
I knew money was not the ultimate need,
He should have something spiritual upon which to feed.
God had given me a chance to put His word into play,
And I with self-righteous indignation let it slip away.
I wanted to select with whom I would share,
I thought I'd always been just and fair.

I wanted to get that picture out of my head so much,
Remove the desire to reach out and touch.
Before I knew why or how, I had returned to that street,
But the man who had moved my heart had changed his seat.
It confirmed to me that opportunity does not knock twice,
My hesitation was exacting a mighty high price.
God has not given me His word to hide,
Nor is who comes in my path for me to decide.
Now I realize if I have an answer to give,
I must share it that my brother may live.

I always thought I had nothing to give,
Especially when I saw how others live.
My background is not from society's top,
From the beginning Mom was separated from Pop.

We couldn't afford the latest fad,
We were thankful for whatever we had.
According to the stories the media told,
I should have given up, let my hand fold.

But my mother was the one who set the tone.
She would not leave me or my aspirations alone.
I was told I was not sediment but pure cream,
She gave inspiration and dared me to dream.

Once I looked at my self instead of circumstances,
The world became an open book full of chances.
But the job is not done when we individually see;
We must help to set our brothers free.

Don't stand on the outside and wonder why,
Get in there, touch and help them try.
This is how we can achieve the most,
Don't hit a plateau and try to coast.

You must know that we all have something to give,
Remember love is essential for everyone to live.

I didn't understand the magnitude of the problem that existed,
How our values had become so demented and twisted.
When did we start to give priority to material things,
And leave moral issues to television to bring.

Oh I understand the economics of the matter,
That it takes two incomes to climb that ladder.
But of responsibility we will not be relieved,
When we cause an entire generation to be underachieved.

This generation needs our foundational support,
They don't need another friend with which to sport.
Are you afraid your mandatory directions
Will take time and cause for juvenile objections.

Well when that child became yours
That's the role you agreed to bore.
It's time to step up strong and bold,
So a well-adjusted adult you could mold.

We know exactly what we want our children to be,
The problem is they emulate what they see.
So next time you say from where did that come?
Think how old was I when I started to crack my gum?

These kids are trying so hard to do things right,
But we keep throwing cold water on their light.
They need some adults who are willing to live,
So straight and narrow not one seam will give.

At first that road may be rocky and you may fall,
But we must keep them in line, prepare them for their call.
This is how a kingdom is built, young people who love the Lord,
Gathering and leading their friends on board.

We don't look out for one another anymore,
There doesn't seem to be the same concern as before.
When the neighbors cared about your kids,
And we didn't have to hire babysitters through bids.
I'm not knocking sociological progress,
But it should not mean moral regress;
We must find that common thread,
Before this generation is spiritually dead.
We just don't anymore.

We don't talk to one another anymore,
Seems like we're always reaching for a new door.
Don't want to sit back and reflect,
Just want to move on to what's next.
I'm not asking anyone to stand still,
I wouldn't want to cause a financial ill,
Just thought some sincere conversation,
Might take the place of future probation.
We just don't anymore.

We don't touch one another anymore,
We're afraid to let anyone to the core.
For self protection we pretend to be on the move,
Firmly fixed into some professional groove.
I'm not suggesting any kind of career delay,
I wouldn't want you to lose an increase in pay,
Just thought a tender heartfelt caress
Might keep a few names out of the press.
We just don't anymore.

We don't love one another anymore,
We think love can be bought in a store.
We look to the package size and price,
To determine whether the inside is nice.
I'm not saying buy only what you need
I wouldn't want the economy to recede,
But have you considered spending time
And doing something without a dime.
We just don't anymore.

There are those who feel let down,
Because their fathers chose not to hang around.
Either that or Dad chose not to participate,
Even when son tried to fully cooperate.
Naturally they could not reveal their true pain,
They didn't want their mothers to feel any disdain.
But they felt doomed from the start,
So why become involved and do their part.

Those feelings of paternal abandonment
Could not be removed no matter how much others spent.
They proceed through life while their shoulders have a chip.
Thinking someone is going to pay for their parents relationship.
But when the debt is finally counted,
It is upon their own tab that it is mounted.
What they must know is that while Mom and Dad did the act,
The reason they're here is God's plan, and that's a fact.

You see we all play a part in this game,
And God has assigned our roles by name.
He knew you while your dad was still a kid,
And had determined just where and when you would do your bit.
So while our natural parents' love can not be discounted,
Through Christ the absence of it can be surmounted.
Put those things over which you have no control
In God's hands and get on with meeting your goal.

They told us not to set our goals too high
Because we could never do anything but menial labor;
After all we're Black men's children.
We don't want you to fail, so don't try.
Their story was so compelling we even began to believe it,
And teach our children as though it were true.
Their perception of us, our perception of ourselves,
Has caused us, as a people, to never be free of the
Bondage that brought us to this land.
That bondage is leading us to destruction.
Now is the time to set aside that yoke.
God has demonstrated His faith and trust in the Black man.
Why can't we accept this by faith
And believe we play a part in His plan.
With this understanding the yoke will be gone.
Where Jesus is Lord, satan can not survive.
So accept Jesus Christ as your savior,
Reset your goals in His name and there is no mountain too high.

She had so much to give, yet no one to give it to.
She dreamed of the perfect world;
Where hugs are returned and dreams are shared,
But who had time for that foolishness.

Then he came into her life,
She was sixteen, he was seventeen;
And he brought meaning into her life,
So she thought.

They dreamed together and made plans for a bright future.
It seemed only natural when he asked if she loved him
That her reply be expressed in physical terms.
After all a love that strong could only be forever.

She didn't understand that his forever
Meant only as long as he had no responsibility.
So when their child was born he was not there.
She felt so forsaken and lost.

Now there was a child looking to her for a perfect world,
And all she had was shattered dreams.
There was nothing on which to hold;
She was standing on sinking sand.

Then one night in her loneliness
She found a tattered old Bible;
She opened that book and became captivated by God's word;
Here was her perfect world, how many times had she passed it.

Now when her child looks up to her with wonder in his eyes,
She will have his answer,
For she can share the greatest love known to man,
And a world of endless possibilities in Jesus Christ.

I saw a young Black man with his head held high,
He pranced like a peacock, so I asked him why,
He said he's been fashioned after a Priest and a King,
Of this he was so sure he said, "Let the mountaintops ring."

Of course others try to tell me I'm not very smart,
The best I'll ever do is to sell apples from a shopping cart.
But I set my goals like my forefather Nimrod,
Heaven bound, so upon me no one will trod.

They try to tell me my values are not right,
All I ever want is to sneak around in the night.
But then I think of the valor of Bethsheba's man,
How when he had a chance to run, he chose to stand.

Some even try to say I don't treat my woman nice,
Leave her or beat her, not once, but twice.
But that is not how I was designed to be,
My women is my glory, my children the fruit of my tree.

This young Black man had so much to say,
I had to ask him how he got that way.
He said the light you see is from above,
I'm walking and living in God's love.

I saw a woman mourning the lost of her son today.
She'd given him up to the world and he was taken away.
She thought the thing of which he had become part
Was too big to fight so she did not start.

Instead she accepted and loved what he was;
Figured it best not to ask what he does.
When she spiritually gave up on her son
Is actually when his future was done.

God has never given up on any one of us,
That's why we're still here able to fight and fuss.
What He did was put His Son in the gap,
Until we can break free of the worldly trap.

We must stop trying to put blame elsewhere,
Always claiming life is not fair.
Blaming the White man for slavery,
Yet voluntarily keeping our minds unfree;
Blaming society for our share of the pie,
Yet not always willing to give life a try.
Black men blame their women for the role they play,
Which causes the blame upon their children to lay;
Black women have given up and won't take time,
Especially when that man is without a dime.

I know old habits are hard to let go,
And even more so when they are all you know.
But I have an answer to put in their place,
It has to do with resting in God's grace.
Jesus has said thru Him victory we can claim,
So we need not search where to place the blame.
Anything that happened yesterday or today,
Jesus by His resurrection has taken them away.
He's given us a foundation upon which to rely,
So to excuses we should say good-bye.

Now I know these words are easier said then done,
We must place our reliance in the Greater One;
We should continually remove any areas of doubt,
Get on with life, let God help you figure it out.
Then unlike you have ever done before,
You can say "I don't need an excuse anymore."

I wanted to live life in obscurity,
Wanted to do God's will privately.
I didn't want to be center of attention,
Didn't even want honorable mention.
I didn't want to have a call,
Thought the pressure might cause my fall.

But then His anointing fell on me,
Took away my tranquility.
I could no longer sit back and watch
While satan added another notch.
I had to take a stand,
It's all part of God's master plan.

I've given God authority with this life,
To fight apathy, depression or strife.
He's not given me secrets galore,
He's only shown me what to thank Jesus for.
But my life I live to make a difference in
The world, family, foe and friend.

When these poems started to come
It made me question just where from.

I knew it was not my intellectual ability,
I was simply being used as a utility.

God has caused these words to flow,
Wanted to give a new gift here below.

His sentiments He wanted to simply portray,
And not create new areas of gray.

He knows the words and tone may entice
Those who usually would not think twice.

This opportunity He put in a different form
In hopes new Christians might readily conform.

But we should not think it simple play,
God wants our conversion right now, today.

I always knew God had a plan for me,
I could look at the gifts I was given and clearly see.
This was something I just naturally believed,
I sat back and waited for instructions to be received.
But then I felt God in my life begin to move,
Pointing out areas that I needed to improve.
This made me know my time was getting near,
It made me worry, I was starting to fear.
Dear God what if I'm not up to the task?
My child I give you the things required for what I ask.
He said My grace is sufficient to do all things.
It's what My Son used and He's King of Kings.
So now I know it is sufficient for what I must do,
And it's God's word which is getting me through.

I came to you all down and out,
Looking for something yet full of doubt.
I was always able to draw my own conclusion,
Then there came so much confusion.
Blindly led by every wind and doctrine,
Allowing society my values to define.
But then, Your word caused a change in me!
Removed the scales that I might see.
Now I live to do Your will,
And my heart is calm and still;
Because in You I found a friend,
For now, forever, until the end.

As I grow stronger in Your word,
I feel freedom, like a bird.
My every need is in Your hand;
Which gives me strength to take my stand,
To remove those yokes and quit that game;
And live to glorify Your holy name.
I say, Your word has caused a change in me!
Removed the scales that I might see.
Now I live to do Your will,
And my heart is calm and still;
Because in You I found a friend,
For now, forever, until the end.

That I might be pleasing to Your sight,
I choose to live my life right.
Love my brother as You command,
Follow Your every way and demand.
Give up that worldly thing
And walk that walk just like I sing.
Your word has caused a change in me!

It was hard to believe God loved me
    after all I never felt love before,
Standing in the shadows most times
    afraid to enter the door.
But then the change I felt in my heart
    I could not explain,
Until I understood that God
    operates on a higher plane.

When I accepted Jesus into my life
    and said you are my Lord;
Then God gave me His Spirit
    as a new survival cord.
Now it is His word that
    determines my every direction,
And this I can accept because
    I believe in Jesus's Resurrection.

Intellectually in Jesus I did believe,
It was far-fetched, but I figured no intent to deceive.
I mean the story of a God becoming man for me.
To carry my sins and set me free.

Then By God's omnipotent design,
Jesus entered this contrite heart of mine.
I saw in old testament times, they knew a child would be born,
To save us all and it happened one Christmas morn.

I saw what that Child's life has meant,
That there's no need for our lives to be twisted and bent.
He's given us power over life and death,
But we allow satan to perpetrate a theft.

We let satan tell us Jesus is dead,
That His resurrection has been totally misread.
We allow satan to steal our joy,
Has us seeking pleasure in some man-made toy.

But this is not how it was supposed to be,
Not when your sins are taken away and you've been set free.
So I looked for the answer in the word from above,
Found the power I needed is in God's love.

The first step is to let Jesus in,
Then receive His Spirit, this is the answer my friend.

The world gave me success
  measured by education,
But could not give internal peace
  that came with salvation.

The world gave me success
  measured by things,
But could not give love
  that came from the King of Kings.

The world gave me success
  measured by all my peers,
But could not give eternal life
  that came from God upstairs.

The world gave me success
  measured by my position,
But had no forgiveness
  without some condition.

The world gave me success
  and told me to choose,
And that's why I chose
  my Savior's shoes.

I love Jesus with all my heart,
It was Him that gave me a new start.
He is in charge of my development,
Since I went to the altar to repent.
He goes to the Father for me in prayer;
He surrounds me in a loving atmosphere.

And if I will in His name ask,
Then it becomes His holy task,
To see that the will of the Father is done;
This He accepts and considers fun.
He does this to glorify the Father's name,
He's not seeking self-serving fame.

He's filled me full of holy fire,
Removed all that worldly desire,
Caused me to be divinely fulfilled,
And my enemies permanently stilled.
So you see it is to Him that I give honor and praise,
Because this is a new child He has raised.

When God is looking for someone to do His will,
I hope I'm in position to fit the bill;
When satan says to God, "Your servants are lacking
   and this I can prove."
I hope God says, "There is one you can try
   who I know will not move."

I'm willing to give my life in the biblical sense,
According to God's word and not under just any pretense.
It is only reasonable service that this we should do,
After all look what God has done for me and you.

When I started this christian walk
The people around me started to talk.
It's not that they wanted me to backslide,
But most had already judged my inside.

And according to their standards I was fine,
After all with the world I was in line.
I had always done what was expected,
So my true discontent was never detected.

But as I grew older
And my heart waxed colder,
I knew that something must be done,
So I turned to the Lord, the Greater One.

He gives me the strength under which to abide
And a light impossible to hide.
Now that they see from the world I'm estranged,
Their conversations have sincerely changed.

They want to know what's brought me peace,
And caused me anxiety and stress to release.
I tell them in my Lord I find delight,
I no longer look for a cause or a fight.

I'm looking at things from a new perspective,
It has to do with my spiritual introspective,
I no longer feel victimized by circumstances,
But rather I see situations as victory chances.

When they try to put me down they don't understand,
Without ducking or dodging their punches won't land.
God has surrounded me with an impenetrable shield.
This is what sending Jesus to the cross did yield.

He's given me solid ground on which to plant my feet,
And has reserved for me a holy seat.
It is in this understanding that I confidently rest,
And has me always expecting God's best.

I told my friend I accepted Christ, I'd be going to a new place;
I heard the snicker and saw the skepticism on her face.
Oh, but the exhilaration and excitement I felt,
I thought even her hard heart would melt.

I showed her the same thing I saw,
Even told her about the change in Paul.
But it all seemed to pass right by,
There was an emptiness in her eye.

It was then that I realized it was not me,
Who could bring about the change I wanted to see.
I needed to put it in my Lord's hand,
And trust and wait and understand.

At times I wonder how my sisters have made it this far,
So many abused and battered or alone with an emotional scar.
I think of Sister Sally whose baby died at two;
Some say it was a cold, others say the flu.
But there is agreement that it did not have to be;
If her old man paid a doctor instead of the bar at 14th and T.

As my heart wept for Sister Sally I asked, "Why still to try?"
She said, "I depend upon the Lord to hear my cry."
She stood boldly, strong and tall;
I know my God is there whenever I call.
My sister, you think womanhood means passive and meek.
But child being a woman can't be done by anyone who is weak.

They talk about my old man, but he does his best;
He doesn't turned to Jesus to guide him to that perfect rest.
But Sister I cannot allow that to destroy what I know,
I just pray that the seed I plant will take root and grow.
The things she said made me think about the seeds I've sown.
Will they bring life: Are they how I want to be known?

My thoughts then turned to Sister Ann's son,
He's the drug dealer you know the one.
Oh Sister Ann claims he's so precious and fine,
I thought because his profits kept her dressed in the latest design.

As my heart condemned Sister Ann I asked, "Why not try?"
She said, "I depend upon the Lord to hear my cry."
She stood boldly, strong and tall;
I know my God is there whenever I call.
My Sister, you think womanhood means passive and meek.
But child being a woman can't be done by anyone who is weak.

I know what they say about my son and me,
But I had to turn that over to the Trinity.
I've given that boy everything I knew to give,
I believe he will turn to the Lord when he's ready to live.
The things she said made me wonder what I had to give,
To make sure my sisters and brothers knew a better way to live.

My thoughts then turned to Sister Carrie,
The one who just can't find anyone to marry.
There have been many suitors one right after the other,
But none seem to want her for their children's mother.

As my heart felt for Sister Carrie I asked, "Why still try?"
She said, "I depend upon the Lord to hear my cry."
She stood boldly, strong and tall;
I know my God is there whenever I call.
My Sister, you think womanhood means passive and meek.
But child being a woman can't be done by anyone who is weak.

I know people have made me the talk of the town,
But getting married isn't reason to accept a clown.
The man that I marry must have Jesus as his source,
I'm not allowing some fool to get me off course.
The things Sister Carrie said were scriptural and sound,
And caused me to check the solidity of my ground.

My look at my sisters lives has made me see,
How dependent we are on others to define who we should be.
But when you allow Christ to be your center
Those deceptions and misconceptions can not enter.
You can stand boldly, strong and tall;
Knowing the Lord will hear your cry whenever you call.

-Dedicated to the Women of Christian Tabernacle for
Women's Day 1991

I was reading the Bible just to be edified,
Trying to keep my spiritual side satisfied.
When I came to the story of Abraham almost sacrificing his son,
Didn't he know Sarah was too old to have another one.
So I said to the almighty, omnipotent God above,
That Abraham wasn't too bright good thing he had your love.
Then I read about Moses leading those people into the Red Sea.
Did he think it was a wading pool that only came to his knee.
So I asked God, was Moses the best you could find,
What didn't anyone back then use their logical mind?
Finally I read of Joshua marching around that wall.
I'm not questioning tactics, but soldiering was not his call.
So I said to God, was Joshua mentally all right,
I mean everyone knows the best time to attack is late at night.

God said, you're reading about My children who lived to obey,
The ones who waited on my voice and did it no other way.
IT WAS BY FAITH that Abraham prepared to sacrifice his son.
He didn't question from where he would get another one.
IT WAS BY FAITH that Moses led them into the Red Sea.
You see Moses believed in God, yes Moses believed in Me!
IT WAS BY FAITH that Joshua marched round and round.
He didn't doubt for a second that the wall would tumble down.
And this is what I ask of My children today,
But you can't imagine how hard it is to find a group to obey.
I have some who can walk that line a little while,
I'm looking for marathoners who are consistent mile after mile.
Then I have those who get on their knees and pray,
Asking Me to just this one time let them do it their way.

What My children have got to understand
Is I'll call on the rocks if necessary to complete My plan.
Tell them to get on with what they were told by me to do.
My children know My voice they won't confuse me and you.
But tell them right now to get into place,
I don't want to leave anyone here when I withdraw My grace.
I could tell by the words He spoke this was no joke,
God is getting ready to open the heavens and retrieve His folk.

My christian walk has Christ at the center.
I'm not focused on some natural mentor.
Oh, our spiritual leaders are fine,
But I always have Christ on my mind.

God chooses the vessel to use,
So let man not the roles confuse.
His trust is placed in those willing to serve.
Yes our respect they surely deserve,
But it was Christ who paid for my salvation;
And it's not sold by some religious corporation.

It is Christ I want to know.
It is Him I want to see in the final show.
So if I can't get some man's okay,
It won't cause my walk to sway.

The devil tried a sneak attack,
Came at me from my back.
He used a dear, dear friend,
One who had pledged love until the end.

Oh, I'm not going to say it didn't hurt,
After all he dredged up a lot of dirt.
But I took my Lord at His word,
When He said He'd fight my enemies 1st, 2nd or 3rd.

So in my distress when I called His name,
My enemies came up lame.
The devil can't find a place in me to rest,
God has put the Greater One in me and will accept any test.

Hey new Christian do you want to talk
About your newly started walk;
About how some days you ride the crest,
Then the next day there is heaviness in your chest;
About how you feel you're touching the sky,
Then the next minute an airplane couldn't help you fly.

This phenomenon is not unique,
The devil is coming at you because you're weak.
He tries to make you think you've been benched,
Before in God's word you become entrenched.
He knows if he can shake your confidence,
He can probably keep you on the fence.

And if you try to walk that line,
He will defeat you eight times out of nine.
So anytime you feel real low
Take your Bible and to God's word you should go.
Study to show yourself approved,
And to tell the devil you can't be moved.

Each
time
I
remember
where
I
was
before
I
knew
Jesus
Christ
as
my
Lord
and
Savior;
I
realize
that
miracles
are
still
being
performed
today.

My God is INFINITE
  but I make Him finite.

My God is LIMITLESS
  but I limit Him.

My God is ALL MIGHTY
  but I make Him powerless.

My God is ALIVE
  but I make Him dormant.

Oh, but that my heart would catch up with my head.

I didn't understand why I could get no satisfaction,
Seemed like my mind was divided into a multitude of factions.
Going from one job to the next for money,
But still had not found my milk and honey.
Always seeking a new romance,
Trying not to awake from that perpetual trance.
Buying new toys and all kinds of stuff,
But never really getting enough.
I was trying to fulfill an internal need
By succumbing to my external greed.

It was just recently that I realized peace is not achieved
Through the number or size of the dollars received.
I had to do a sincere soul search,
Figured the best place to start would be church.
I'd been under a wrong impression from year to year;
The physical structure is not the reason Jesus was here.
He's given each of us the cross to focus on,
That through our lives wondrous gifts would spawn.
The only thing He wants in return,
Is for us to walk such that others would yearn
To know how to obtain this gift of love,
And build a relationship with God above.

I talked to Jesus the other day,
We discussed why so many stray.
I told Him about the lore of the street,
And new drug habits difficult to beat.
I told Him about big government's delay,
And how businesses are not willing to pay.
I told him that now kids are on there own,
And that's why they are acting grown.
I went on to explain how the price of rent,
Had most of us emotionally spent.
But for each reason I thoughtfully gave,
He'd say, "That's no reason to misbehave."

I walked this earth in the form of man,
So these conditions I understand.
I know the desire for riches and fame,
I was offered a kingdom if I'd bow to satan's name.
I know hunger makes the body weak,
And the flesh is that which satan seeks.
But God has given you spiritual food,
That gives you the power to refuse.
You see satan knows he is doomed to fail,
For the power inside you can whip his tail.
And that is why he tries to keep hidden,
The gospel which God has had written.

He then proceeded to tell just how and why,
Upon God's word we must learn to rely.
You see God gives us a simple plan,
To ensure the righteousness of man.
He ask that you accept Jesus as the way,
Through confession and belief every day.
He ask that you show your love for Him
By loving your brothers, all of them.
And then with boldness He wants you to witness,
Of the power of His in obtaining true fitness.
By complying with all of God's wishes.
He will bestow upon you unknown riches.

I had become comfortable living life at the edge,
I figured if danger could be seen it would be easier to hedge.
I realize because of my closeness sometimes I got burn,
But there was just too much going on to give that concern.
Then into my heart Jesus did enter
And He told me He wanted me dead center.
My response was I'm not sure that is what I should do,
I won't have anything to hold onto.
Jesus graciously extended His hand
And I knew beside Him, He was asking me to stand.

I saw him from the otherside of the room,
My heart went pitter patter, my pressure went zoom.
His eyes twinkled, his smile slightly downward bent,
I knew he must have been heaven sent.

So to my single days I was ready to bid adieu,
Until I asked the question and he said, "Jesus Who?"
The boy didn't even know who Jesus was,
Let alone what the resurrection does.

So I began to explain about the Son of Man,
Tried to tell him for his life God had a plan.
He looked me straight in the eye,
And said, "I know all the answers why not give me a try?"

Why that knucklehead was so wrapped up in himself,
At times I thought I was talking to a leprechaun or an elf.
First I decided in my singleness to rest,
Then I put my witness to a test.

I prayed for that man and told him of a life,
One void of envy, confusion and strife.
It took a while but he began to see,
He started shouting, "Thank God I've been set free."

Today that man has taken a wife.
They have three kids and live a glorious life.

Each day when I'd wake there'd be new problems to face,
Most times I couldn't pay anyone to take my place.
The car would break down and a new one was too much money,
All my friends and love ones were acting funny.
When I was looking for someone to just give me a hug,
You'd think I'd asked for a wall-to-wall oriental rug.
Before I could even explain my plight,
One by one they have taken flight.
This made me question just why I'm here,
When I can't even get my family to care.

Then a man I hardly knew,
Gave me advice on what to do.
He suggested that I let Jesus into my heart,
Give Him my problems and let Him pull them apart.
Now I'd heard this before, two times maybe three,
And I always knew it wasn't for me.
Eventually I always figure my own problems out,
I have above average ability and little self doubt.
The man replied keep thinking your doing it by yourself;
You're probably think you don't need that Bible on your shelf.

God looks over each one of us and does it so well,
That when He steps in you can't even tell.
Then I started to think, if God wanted to show His concern,
Seems like He'd put out the fire before we got burn.
The man was ready with his reply,
And went into great detail to explain just why.
You see God has given man dominion in this realm,
We must give Him authority to take over the helm.
When we decide to live according to God's will,
He explained that's when life begins for real.

This man went on for hours;
Telling how God had given him all his desires.
He wanted me to know that God wants a relationship
With each of us regardless of our kinship.
He became so involved with my state of affairs,
I asked him, just why do you care?
He said my love for the Lord is so great,
That I don't want anyone to miss the Kingdom's gate.
I could clearly see that in the Lord he did rejoice,
And this is how I came to make my choice.

I prayed to my God above,
For a mighty touch of His love.
It seemed He'd gone away,
My blue sky was turning gray.

Then I heard Him say, I gave My Son that you might live,
What more do you want Me to give?
I put My Spirit on your inside,
That to all truth He would be your quide.
Then daily I supply whatever you need,
So why can't I get you to follow instead of lead.

I knew what my Lord said to me was true,
But it seemed like everything was coming unglued.
I was looking for some mighty sign to show
That the one in control was the God I know.

Is there a greater sign that I could give
Then that My Son died that you might live.
Don't you know you've been washed by the water of My word,
Through My cleansing your vision's been unblurred.
But now it's up to you by faith to believe
So that each one of My blessings you may receive.

It's just that sometimes You seem so far away.
It feels like You don't hear me when I pray.
Did I offend My God that I love by something I didn't do,
Don't You understand just how much I need you.

My child I understand exactly what you say,
I also need your fellowship everyday.
So you must know that I'll always be there,
Trying desperately to get your ear.
But you build up those invisible wall,
Then look for any excuse to fall.

Your word I try so hard to obey,
But things just come and pull me away.
How many times can I count on You to forgive,
When a better life I know I should live.

It is your heart that is My concern,
Once it's in line the rest you'll easily learn.
But don't think this gives an excuse to sin.
Just always know upon Me you can depend.
And remember I gave My Son that you might live,
A greater gift there is not to give.

Sometimes God gives us a message to share,
But how often does it hit the intended ear.

We tell our Christian friends instead of non-believers,
But were they really the intended receivers.

We testify of God's true power,
But only from our protected ivory tower.

Then we question the non-believer's doubt,
But we haven't told him what this walk is about.

He may not know that Jesus is the way,
And God had given you just what to say.

Next time you start to speak in Jesus' name
Consider whether you're playing some christian game.

I had decided to ignore my family connection,
And my family raised no noticeable objection.
It seemed the whole world had overcome,
And those people were sitting on their thumbs.
I was not going to let them hold me back,
Thought I'd be better off without their flack.
Then out of social consideration,
I attended a reunion of my relations.
For the first time I sat and listened
To the stories they told and my insides glistened.
My ancestors wanted the same things as the rest,
And the foot they put forward was always their best.
But I had allowed society make me feel shame,
Because we carried some slave owner's name.
But the roots upon which I was laid,
Were nothing short of a top notch grade.
I don't think I was out there alone,
Thinking my family I had out grown.
There are more of us who need to look back,
And allow our families to get us on track.
The good thing is the family is always there,
Waiting for you to get your act in gear.
They reach out and love so much,
You wonder why you ever loss touch.
And once the family is reunited,
Foundationally you will be ignited.

Learned men question the Holy Spirit's work,
Some say He may be a passe quirk.
Some denominations think His power unneeded,
I guess their enemies are all defeated.
But God is not an indian giver,
The Holy Spirit is here to deliver.

To understand what you should know,
You must appreciate the Godhead flow.
The Godhead is a tripartite affair, but really one;
Consisting of the Holy Spirit, Father and Son.

Now God the Father is our creator,
Maker, defender, call him perpetrator.
Now God the Son made the ultimate sacrifice,
To ensure our salvation He agreed to come here twice.
Now God the Holy Spirit followed the Son,
And is here until the "Body" is completely done.

God the Father talked directly to the old testament saint;
God the Son used the disciple His story to paint;
But God the Holy Spirit is here today,
And can help you detect when you're about to stray.

He helps God's children to realize their gifts
And through that internal rubble He continually sifts.
If upon Him you learn to rely,
You can experience that spiritual high.
But His existence we should not ponder or doubt,
He is the only part of the Godhead currently out.

We spend a lot of time dwelling on our past deeds,
Be they good or bad, upon them we should not continually feed.

When we repented of the sins we committed
God forgave us and promised to forget it.

In God's kingdom there is work to be completed,
There's no time to wallow in what's been deleted.

The devil wants to keep us in the past,
Make us feel unworthy, unable to be steadfast.

God has told us our slate is wiped clean,
If they pop-up again tell the devil "I don't know what you
mean".

I believed people were what they said they were,
Then my experience in the church caused my vision to blur.
I found there is a difference between religion and spirituality,
And what people say has very little to do with reality.
I further found that there are those who try to use their pew,
As a place from which judgment of the many is made by a few.

I have learned not to be bothered by them,
And rest in the fact that I am seeking after Him.
I just wish we could learn not to judge,
And make people feel a commitment they must fudge;
But accept each one from where he is at,
And make sure we don't allow anyone to hold us back.
By giving each one this unconditional love,
We will find favor from God above.

I thought salvation was tied to church folks,
So I gave up the world and put on a religious yoke.
My praise and worship depended on which friends were around;
I knew I'd been lost, didn't realize I was not found.

I joined the church and immediately started to give,
But I did nothing to change the way I live.
I knew exactly what words to say,
But there was something lacking when I would pray.

This relationship I have must be seen,
In the way I live, if you know what I mean.
God is not looking for self-righteous testimony,
He can easily detect an insincere phony.

We get so caught up in trying to prove spiritually,
That we lose sight with actual reality.
God has something specifically designed for us to do,
But He looks at your heart before He places His trust in you.

What we must do is totally submit,
Give God our heart and ask Him to change it.
Then that desire to let others see you grow
Will be replaced by what you know you know.

God has given me the foundation
For my spiritual supplication.
This should not cause you to be perplex,
It's well documented in His biblical text.
He told Peter upon this rock My church I'll build,
And gave him teachings new converts to yield.

The church is the "body" and Christ the "head",
And it was for this arrangement that Jesus bled.
This church is not some building standing tall,
But rather He placed His temple inside us all.
Now it is our job to go out and preach
The gospel to everyone we can reach.

I don't let the opinions of others
   influence my thought.
My approval or agreement
   cannot be bought.
If you freely determine
   what things mean,
And do not from the group
   your values glean
There are those who will try
   to control your mind
By implying new friends
   they will find.
This threat of being
   left out
Is usually what loyalty
   is about.
God has given each of us
   the ability to think.
He does not want you
   into oblivion to sink.
Of the group you may be able
   to be a part,
Just be sure to consult God
   from the start.
Depend upon His will
   for your direction,
And be prepared for
   the group's rejection.
Your willingness to be steadfast
   and go it alone,
Is directly related to how far
   in His word you have grown.

A friend is a precious thing to have
Their comfort can be a spiritual salve.

A friend will point out when you're off track,
And patiently wait until you get back.

A friend has your best interest at heart,
And in your life takes an active part.

A friend is not just someone with which to hang,
Or sit around and talk about any old thang.

Friendship should spark your personal growth,
Then the achievements of one can be shared by both.

I turned my back on what I knew was right,
Became distracted by the things of the night.
It always looked like they were having fun over there;
I figured a little detour, God would not care.
But I notice as my involvement increased,
Things in my life started to become deceased.
God had given us a rule to apply,
When you sin something is sure to die.

I saw my personal relationships changed,
People around me started to act deranged.
I could no longer professionally perform,
My life had become one continuous storm.
My health took a turn for the worst,
My heart felt like it was going to burst.
My involvement became so deep,
I didn't realize I'd lost my peaceful sleep.

I then started to associate what God said,
To what I saw and knew I'd been had.
You see God has given us a warning,
To prevent our having to go into mourning;
Advising the wages of sin is death for sure,
And it is something you'll just have to endure.
But it is simple to get back on track,
Return to God's word and never look back.

An Evangelist came to town to speak,
Out of curiosity I went to take a peak.
Her words were sharp and curt,
Around the issues she did not skirt.
She said Christians must get their lives in toll,
Salvation is intended to make our lives whole.

She spoke of the spirit, mind and body being one,
It is through Christ that this can be done.
It is hard to see what you profess,
When you own life is in a mess.
We must exhibit the truth and love,
Which we claim from the Father above.

The world is continually looking at us,
So why do we internally fight and fuss.
We must ensure our concerns are intact,
Our lives should be nothing less than exact.
This is how souls are won to glory,
What is seen should tell the story.

Now is the time to seek you clemency,
Can't you feel that sense of urgency.
Jesus has said He will come as a thief in the night,
There will be no time to plan your flight.

Some say this is something tomorrow to think about,
They don't understand and they will be left out.
Then there will be those who say "Jesus I loved you a lot",
And Jesus will turn to the Father and say "I'm afraid not".

He will judge your true heart's condition,
Which is not necessarily your churchical position.
But He's given the answer on how to get in line.
You may want to refer to Romans 10:9.

Confess by mouth and believe in your heart,
This will get you a fresh new start.
But He's not looking for arbitrary repentance,
He knows the meaning behind each spoken sentence.

He wants you to step forward for the right reason,
Understanding to the world it's considered treason.
But He will give you the character to be bold,
So that your salvation and righteousness you may hold.

And those who have accepted His salvation,
He wants your lives to be a righteous demonstration,
So that each one of our brothers would see
The true meaning of a life that is free.

I plan to make God's final Call,
I ain't playing around with y'all.
You can shuck and jive all you want,
But with salvation I do not taunt.

My Lord has told us just what He'll do.
That's good enough for me and I hope you to.
He's going to take the keys of death and hell
And lock satan in his own personal jail.

Satan will have company if you don't take care,
For anyone who takes his mark will get his share.
But for those who are willing to submit,
God has planned the ultimate "it".

The lion and the lamb will play together,
Sickness and hunger gone forever.
Of this paradise I want to partake,
And will do what's necessary that call to make.

People have developed a false sense of security,
Assuming God has changed His definition of purity.
They think because society now operates in a sexual mode,
God has redefined His moral code.
But this is simply a misconception,
God has been the same since our inception.

We try to justify and condone our lifestyle;
But God hasn't given an inch, He knows we'd take a mile.
We want to believe God has changed His temperament,
That He'll be a little easier in final judgement.
But God told Malachi "I am Lord I change not."
The validity of His rules is what should be taught.

Your moral decisions should be made
Based upon the foundation biblically laid;
And not some new social trend,
Which the world has decided to defend.
This should cause you great relief,
It gives you something unmovable in which to plant your belief.

This is written to give you an appreciation
For the "body's" interconnecting operation.
You see God gave three categories of gifts to men;
And each category has specific types within.
Functional, perfecting and protecting are the categories;
And they all operate to bring God the glory.

Members have at least one functional gift.
To prevent the "body" from going adrift.
No one gift is considered best,
Each one is dependent on the rest.
When members contribute their fair share,
The "body" operates like a well-oiled gear.

Then you have the perfecting, gifts given to some.
These gifts require ordination or will remain mum.
They are provided to bring the body to fruition,
To keep each member in his rightful position.

Now the protecting gifts which match their name,
Are the ones satan has made part of his game.
Satan knows that by these gifts the members are mused,
Therefore he copies them to keep the saints confused.
But God has given us the power to reveal,
When it is satan who is doing the deal.

Part of understanding how these gifts flow,
Is knowing that God chooses where they go,
He has not left the decision to man,
But made it part of His plan.
So you see each gift has its place,
To be used with the sufficiency of God's grace.

I knew a women who had two sons,
One kept his mind stayed on God the Greater One.
The other was all entwined in the world's affairs,
God was the furthest thing from his daily cares.

But his momma prayed for that boy everyday,
Refused to let the world take her baby away.
As time went by the boy said, "I can't do it no more."
He showed up broken hearted, weeping at his mother's door.

She took him in, no need to ask why.
It had to be Jesus who answered her cry.
Now that women has two sons working for the Lord.
Her household is at peace, in one accord.

So you see my child, pray for your friend,
That her heart would be softened to let Jesus in.
Once you have turned her over to one above,
Soon she will be walking in God's love.

I was embarrassed to go to the Father in prayer,
I couldn't get my thoughts and my words in gear.
I especially felt unworthy after hearing others pray,
They must have practiced just what to say.
I confided in a friend of mine,
That I could not get my prayer life in line.
She told me to just say what was in my heart,
Stop trying to sound spiritually smart.
No one understood that after all God had done for me,
I felt the least I could do was study for a prayer degree.
After much consternation and thought,
I began to see that what is in the heart can not be taught.
So now when I go to the Father for spiritual feed,
I allow His Spirit to take the lead.

I did not pray today because I didn't need anything.
When I woke I saw the sun and I heard the bird sing.
The alarm went off I was not running late,
I didn't need to ask God to get me there by eight.

The car started without a hitch,
I didn't need to ask God, what a switch.
The lights were all in my favor,
So why should I call on my savior.

I arrived at my desk with time to spare,
But then could not understand my despair;
I had not talked to my friend today,
To thank Him for paving the way.

It made me stop and think,
Give God the glory, not just a wink.
I pray that I might communicate,
With my Lord, who keeps me straight.

Why does another's position always seem better than mine?
Why is it when I have eight I always need nine?
I took these questions to my source above,
Told Him my lack of things was making me feel no love.
I knew God was taking care of my need,
But there was something out there tickling my greed.

I guess you think it was pretty bold for me to complain,
But God patiently commenced to explain,
Your love is not tied to a thing,
No matter what you have you're the child of the King.
He said, "I only give you that which you can handle,
In your case be thankful you're not reading by candle."

They wanted to know where I stood,
I always thought on the side of good.

After all I went church week after week,
Gave to the poor, protected the meek.

I thought it sufficient to follow the rules of man,
I had developed my own righteousness plan.

Then the Spirit led me to an altar call;
I was proudly standing tall.

Then the words of the Pastor
Revealed that my heart was made of plaster.

There was a whole lot of work to be done,
But the Holy Spirit had already begun.

Now I look back on those days
And wonder how I managed in that haze.

I now have a Christlike mind,
And my mouth and my heart are aligned.

When I was a child just like you,
My friends told me I should celebrate Christmas like they do.
When they told me about the toys, Santa and all,
I started thinking they've got something on the ball.
So I took this story home to my dad.
Told him if he didn't cooperate I'd be real sad.
He said good then there'll be no reason to ask why,
When I say outta' here with the foolishness, and you start to cry.
He said you see this house serves the Lord,
If you can't cooperate it's time for you to de-board.

It took time to understand why we couldn't have it two ways.
I mean after all Christmas is just one of many days.
Then my father took me in his loving arms,
That's how it starts, we think, one sin what's the harm.
But serving the Lord means one hundred percent.
No time off on holidays, not even during lent.
But this should not cause you to be sad,
What it does is to get the devil real mad.
From that day forward I understood my Dad,
He was right, serving the Lord has made me happy and glad.

I searched for the meaning of Christmas with great resolve,
Decided if I didn't know I shouldn't be involved.
So I asked my friends what Christmas meant,
One told me it was measured by how much was spent.

So to the stores I promptly proceeded,
And with open arms was warmly greeted.
But when my money was no longer there,
They withdrew the offer of Christmas cheer.

Then someone told me I should count the gifts received,
Christmas is when you see how you are really perceived.
Then someone gave me a self-operated per rock.
Does this mean they think my head is a block.

Then someone told me Christmas is an emotion we feel,
Okay now this had to be the real deal.
After all just the thought of it gives me a chill,
Then I remembered for some this is done by a lottery wheel.

Then I turned to a child's wondrous eyes,
And asked him the wherefors and whys.
He said, this is the day we celebrate the gift from above,
You know God gave His Son to show His love.

This gift was given for all mankind,
But we've allowed greed and profit to get entwined.
We must know in our heart that Jesus is the reason;
And let no man pervert this season.

Well this kid was surely on the ball,
Giving the true meaning of Christmas to one and all.
He ended by saying, "It is not just one day,
You must know that Jesus is the only way!"

There's a story that needs to be told
Of a life that could be like gold.
But there is a price to be paid,
Upon the cross you must be stayed.

The crowd may say I don't understand,
You've always been such a worldly man.
But to this take no heed,
Your inward change is guaranteed.

God has promised salvation
To people of every race and nation.
So your fear will be relieved
If you confess by mouth and in your heart believe.

That Jesus is Lord and of a Virgin born,
Died for us, arose on that third morn.
He sits with the Father in these days and times,
And will come again to judge our crimes.

He was here for you and me
To do away with our iniquity.
His life bold, yet humble,
Strewn with temptation, but never a stumble.

And though His works were great and many,
Our promise is that we too can do plenty.
But first we must accept and pray,
For Jesus Christ is the way.

When He left He sent another
To comfort and guide like a mother.
To Him we are directly tied,
Since God is on our inside.

A relationship with Him is a must,
And this your heart must simply trust.
In order to receive God's power pray,
For the Holy Spirit upon you to lay.

And give you strength the devil to deny
To satan this is a punch in the eye.
For satan wants you to think this all a joke,
That he might bind you with his yoke.

But you must know God wants us near
He gave His Son to show He cares.
There's always room in His home,
His children will not be left to roam.

If this cause you to think of your life,
The confusion, disgust or even strife.
Then now is the time don't be a dope,
Accept Jesus Christ He's your hope!

I hope these poems have made you think,
And they're not stuck on a shelf considered wasted ink.
You see there is a message to be extracted,
A plan delivered to keep your life from being distracted.

These are the last days and times,
I am not harping on broken chimes.
There are basic principles that you must embrace,
Or it is God's wrath judgment that you will face.

This is not some threat idly made,
In Revelations it is simply laid.
God is going to pull His church out of here,
Then with the world He will cause great fear.

Why if God could have His way,
Not one of His children would be required to stay.
But just as His world is not now believed,
Those in tribulation will continue to be deceived.

You see we tend to be hardhead,
Easily fooled and readily misled;
Always looking for that pot of gold,
When it's God's light you should behold.

But maybe these poems will cause a change
And a few new hearts will be rearranged.